The Christmas Story: Remembrance

Jeshua ben Joseph

Copyright ©1994 by Judith Coates

ISBN 1-878555-05-7

Published by
Oakbridge University Press
6716 Eastside Drive N.E., Suite 50
Tacoma, WA 98422
(206) 952-3285

Cover and interior design: Thomas Coates
Original artwork: Patrick Corrigan

*Heartfelt thanks to all, seen and unseen,
who have assisted in the preparation
of this book.*

Preface

How does one describe a process of unfoldment which has brought them to a place where the One known as Jeshua ben Joseph, the Christ, borrows the body and speaks in a very dynamic flow of energy, while the "owner" of the body is very much present and yet is the beholder? How does one describe His manner that is at once universal and holy, personal and loving? With humility and wonder.

The present chapter of unfoldment began for me five years ago with the arrival of a manuscript. It was the typewritten copy of *Jesus and Mastership*, the story of Jesus' life as told by Him through automatic writing, scribed by James Morgan. The discourses had come through in the 1970's, and Jim and his wife, Audre', had tried, unsuccessfully, to find a publisher. After Jim passed on in 1978, Audre' continued to treasure the writings, and in 1989, learning that my husband, Tom, and I were interested in channelled material, she sent the manuscript to us. Tom was at that time minister of a metaphysical church and publishing a monthly newspaper containing channelled information. When we read the manuscript, we knew it had to be made available to people, so we decided we would publish it — even though we knew nothing about publishing!

In preparing *Jesus and Mastership* for publication it was my honor to proofread the pages as they were put in form for the printer. I spent many hours reading and re-reading the words of Jesus, and, as I did so, I felt an increasingly close personal relationship with Him. I had known since childhood that He was my Friend and had prayed to Him, but He seemed some distance away, off in the heavens somewhere. Now I could hear Him speaking to me through the pages of the book. He was becoming personally alive for me.

About the same time as we were preparing to publish our first book, Tom and I, along with six other colleagues, were led to incorporate Oakbridge University, a metaphysical vision of higher learning, and as part of the University, we established Oakbridge Chapel, which meets on Sunday mornings. As the Sunday services evolved, I was asked to give the announcements of upcoming classes and workshops being offered in the University during the week, and after a while I felt led to add a bit of inspiration — an affirmation or an uplifting poem, etc. — at the end of the seemingly dry class information. This format continued for some time; then the words came to "Be amongst the people and share from your heart." I didn't know where those words came from, or what they meant exactly, but, okay. I would do the announcements, then leave the lectern and walk down to the first row of seats and share whatever was in my heart — whatever I had read that week that was inspiring, whatever bits of wisdom that had come to me — praying all the while, "God, give me something to say!"

I remember noticing during this time that there was a flow of energy that was palpable, dynamic, while I/we were sharing. And then, at a certain point, it would be like a window shade was descending in front of me (within me?) and the energy changed, and I knew it was time to wrap it up and sit down. What was happening? I didn't know.

We continued in this manner for a year and a half. Then, in the spring of 1993, on a Sunday morning Jeshua announced that He was speaking, that He desired to tell the Easter story in His own words — and that He had been speaking through me for some time.

Concurrent with the evolution of activities of Oakbridge Chapel (nothing ever happens in isolation, does it?), Tom and I were in association with Jon Marc Hammer, who has been channeling Jeshua since the late-1980's, publicly since 1991. We were invited to Marc's first channeling in Tacoma, Washington, and after the Friday night session, Tom was led to record and transcribe the discourses. It was my privilege to proofread the transcriptions. As I sat at my computer two or three evenings a week, reading Jeshua's words on the screen, I began to hear Him speaking to me — not only the words on the screen, but inbetween the lines — very loving, personal messages of Who I am, why I am here, what the world is for, etc. It was/is like being enveloped in a cloud of unconditional Love. So when we came to His revelation that Sunday in March 1993, it came as a surprise — and yet, not surprising. The process has been — and is still — a gradual unfolding, as if He has taken my hand and is gently leading me through a beautiful garden.

Jeshua, through me, is a very dynamic expression, One Who loves to be "amongst the people." He is very personal and interactive, loving and humorous. What you are about to read is taken from transcripts of two evening sessions given in December 1993, in which there was much interaction between Him and the people in the group. Questions (and Answers) asked on those evenings follow the text.

It is my hope that you will enjoy the following and that you will come away enlightened — Lighter as the Heart that we are.

Judith Coates
Tacoma, Washington
September 1994

Beloved one, I would share with you a Remembrance of what has come to be known as the Christmas Story. For you were there. You participated in the birth of one Jeshua ben Joseph. And it is appropriate that we now call to mind and relive the events that happened seemingly so long ago, to celebrate once again a joyous birthing.

2

Beloved and holy and only Child of our Heavenly Father, Child of Light divine, I am the one known as Jeshua ben Joseph — Jesus, you have called me — and it is in great joy that I come to abide with you, as you have chosen to turn the focus of your attention unto me. There is a history that you have asked me to share with you, a story that would be of my birth, of the events surrounding and leading to that celebration, and yet it is your Birth and forthcoming celebration of which we speak. For the Child of God is one, and this is your story.

Once upon a time before time was, the holy Child, the one Child of our Heavenly Father — which is you — thought to set out upon a Journey. In the Adventure of the Child of our Heavenly Father, the adventure that I have called the Dream, you thought to bring forth physicality upon our Holy Mother, the Earth. And when you first appeared, as it would be, upon this plane, you were — and are — a Light being. You were — and are — the Light that touched all of the creations that you manifested with our Holy Mother, the Earth. She, our Mother,

Who gives of Herself the molecules of physicality — known as the dust of the Earth — which you use to form your very bodies, is a Light being, very much alive, very much the Light as you are. And, in conjunction with Her, you brought forth creations upon this plane.

Now, at first, when you manifested physicality, it was very much in a fluid state, very much of the Light.

There was a density of physicality that would define what you would call a body, a vessel, a vehicle, but you knew yourself to be Light. You knew yourself to be the energy that was collecting the molecules unto yourself, and you experimented with different forms of physicality, for you desired to experience all. And in what you would see as time, the focus of attention became even more specific until it was forgotten that you are the Light, that you are the energy that collects what is known as the body unto yourself.

Even as the focus became more specific, even in times when the body was seemingly solid, there was a connection, an opening at the top of the head. This reminder remains today as you will see the newborn and there is the soft spot where the skull has not grown into hardness yet. This was true for all of you — all of us, because I was there as well, in what you would see as a far off time, and yet, if you can relate to that, it is not so far off.

And as you would see time evolving and consciousness evolving, there were those of you who remembered — albeit perhaps in the back of the mind somewhere, as a still small voice that would speak unto you — that there was more. It was a longing to know. There is now a longing to know, a longing to come home and it speaks to you of where your Home is: the Home of the Heavenly Father.

Throughout all civilizations there were ones — they were called the mystical ones — the ones who studied what would be known even in ancient cultures as the holy writings and the ancient scriptures, and there were those who were in tune with the Spirit that you are, and there were those who kept it alive from civilization unto the next civilization. And you, Beloved one, were one who has done this in what you would see as other lifetimes. You have kept the flame alive — the flame of the Light that you are — alive in the consciousness of mankind/womankind.

When the great civilization of Atlantis went through its upheaval, and when the continents were rearranged because of the consciousness of mankind at that time, there were those of you who had foreknowledge that this was going to happen. And some three hundred years before the final descent of Atlantis, there was an emigration that took place. Those who were known as the mystics, those who were in tune with the Heavenly Father and the Light that you are, made trek to a land that is now known as Egypt, taking with you the knowledge and some of the writings for the generations to come.

And out of this history, as you would see it, came a group known as the Brotherhood. It has always been known as the Brotherhood, the Brotherhood of Light — both those that you would see in the unseen realm — now, there is a play on words for you — and those who had chosen to express with the design of the body upon this realm, the Brotherhood. And out of that came the group that was known as Essenes. This was the group that I was born into: my mother, Mary, being an Essene and my Father, Joseph, being a monk at Mount Carmel, the Essene community and monastery.

These were ones who valued the knowledge, the ancient writings and the knowledge of Oneness, the knowledge of the Light that you are, always have been and always will be. And the knowledge was kept alive.

Now, my birth that is so celebrated in your civilization and in your culture — for truly you know that it is not celebrated, and has not been celebrated throughout what you would see as the centuries, by all of your brother and sisters. There are cultures and civilizations that would not even recognize my birth as being anything special. But because you find yourself in this civilization, it is something that is celebrated and is revered for what it symbolizes. Now, my birth — not the individual birth, but the birth of the Messiah — had been foretold down through the ages by the mystical ones, the keepers of the ancient knowledge. They knew the symbolism and the deeper meaning of what had been prophesied, and the birth of the Christ upon this plane was one that was joyously anticipated. In the evolution of time, as you would see it, since my birth the deeper meaning has often been lost, set aside, misunderstood, and I have been worshipped as very God Himself upon this plane. And this is true. I was and I am

— as you are also — very God upon this plane.

The incarnation that you would see as Jeshua ben Joseph was not the only incarnation that I have had upon this plane. If you will receive it, I have been here many other times, expressing. There are the lifetimes recorded in history as Adam, as Melchizedek, as Joshua, as Elisha, as Jeshua — and many others that have not been written about. For truly I have loved our Holy Mother, the Earth, and I have loved the expression of God upon this plane, and there were lifetimes that I spent much as the lifetime that you find yourself in: with the expression of love experienced in relationship with my brothers and sisters, and with a mate and with a family. There were lifetimes of simplicity that have not been recorded in history.

But now I wish to share with you the Remembrance of the Christmas story, so we shall speak of the birth of one Jeshua ben Joseph.

In the Essene community the wisdom of the Elder Brothers and the ancient Scriptures were revered. The ancient Scriptures were carefully preserved, copied for future generations, studied for their symbolism, interpreted, and sometimes debated as to their meaning. There was much symbolism in the ancient writings, and this was passed down from generation unto generation.

My mother, Mary, was one of the ones who was invited to come unto Mount Carmel, the Essene community, to study. As children grew up in an Essene family, or in an Essene community at large, if there was seen an affinity, an alignment, within that child for the mystical knowledge and study, they could be invited to live and study at the monastery at Mount Carmel.

The Essene Brotherhood was not all contained within Mount Carmel. There were many Essenes who lived in the villages, as well, and the Brotherhood was widespread. It was a secret brotherhood in that it was not openly discussed, talked about with all of the people in the countryside, but the ones who were Essenes were known unto each other by various symbols, greetings, by various rituals, I suppose you would call them.

And so, in the villages, if there would be a child who seemed to be of the mystical bent, one who had shown signs that he knew his oneness with the Heavenly Father, he/she would be invited to go unto Mount Carmel and to study, as was my father, Joseph, and as was my mother, Mary.

Mary came unto Mount Carmel at the age of eight. She was one of twelve girls who were invited to come and to study because of her background and because of her gentleness and her purity. She came and studied with the other girls, and boys as well, for there was equality in what you would see as the classes. It was not felt that because you were expressing as the male gender you were automatically more intelligent or more one with the Heavenly Father. Within the Essene community it was understood that the body is as raiment that is put on from one lifetime to another, and you may find in one lifetime that you are as the female body and in the next lifetime you may be expressing as the male body.

So it was not seen that expressing as the male body was more valuable than being as the female body. It was the Spirit and the willingness to know the oneness with our Heavenly Father that was important.

Mary enjoyed being with her teachers and with the other girls and boys at Mount Carmel. She enjoyed the studies, and learning — I would call it remembrance — came easy for her, for there was a natural alignment, a natural knowingness I suppose you would call it, an attunement.

It was known that one of the twelve girls in her class, as you would call it, would be the mother of the long-awaited messiah. This one who lends me her body {Judith} to speak unto you in this way was one who helped in the selection of the twelve. She was one who helped teach the girls, and she was one who wondered, as did the others at Mount Carmel, which one of the twelve would be the vessel that would bear the messiah.

When Mary was twelve, at Passover time, there was a ritual in which all would take part. The rabbis and the priests, as you would see them, came first into the temple that was at Mount Carmel for the morning blessing. And the other monks in what you would see as seniority came in procession next, and the girls — although there was equality — came in at the end of the procession, singing a song of praise.

The convocation was done each morning, but this was a special procession because it was Passover time, and Mary, who was to be my mother, was chosen that morning to lead the procession — which she had done at other times, as well. It was not something new to her, but she had been chosen that morning to be leader and she, because of being leader, also was given the responsibility of choosing the hymn that would be sung — which she did — and it was a hymn of praise, of thanksgiving.

And as the procession of girls came into the temple, there was a loud thunder clap that was heard, and there was darkness as a cloud had passed in front of the sun. And as the cloud passed, it cleared all of the girls except for Mary. And as Mary went up the steps to the altar, it was seen that there was a Presence next to her, and it was seen to be an angel.

Mary did not hear the thunderclap and did not see the cloud that had covered everyone. She felt only joy in her heart, and she climbed the steps to the altar and stood there with the angel, singing and praising our Heavenly Father. And all who saw knew that this one had been chosen.

There was great rejoicing, for the one who would be the mother of the much-anticipated messiah had been selected.

From that time forward Mary was even more intensely instructed in the teachings. She was never left alone, although it was not that she needed to be guarded, but it was that everyone wanted to be in her presence, for there was such a Love that was felt.

For the next two and a half years she studied the Scriptures, she studied what it would mean to be a mother, how a child would be nurtured and brought up in the way of the Essenes, in the way of knowing that he and his Father are one.

When she was close to being fifteen, an angel appeared to her again and spoke unto her, "Blessed art thou among women. Blessed is the fruit of your womb." She accepted these tidings as a blessing but also with great questioning, for the angel told her that she would bear a son who would be the messiah of his people. And she asked how would this be, for she had not known man. And the angel replied that the Holy Spirit would come upon her and a child would be conceived.

Now, unto your world and your thinking in this world, that would be a miracle. It has been called a miracle birth, immaculate conception, a birth only for one who is a miracle upon this plane. And yet, if you will receive it, there are ones in your time upon this plane who also conceive without the cooperation of a male form.

The reason that this can be done — and is done — is because you, as the very energy that you are, are collecting the molecules of physicality unto yourself moment by moment. If you were not doing this, the body would disintegrate and return unto the dust that it is. It is your consciousness **beyond** the conscious mind — although it can be consciously known — it is your consciousness that attracts the molecules into the very shape that you find yourself in.

Because you are the energy of consciousness and you are collecting the molecules of physicality unto you, what you believe can happen, will happen. And because the expectancy was so great in that time — the birth of the messiah was one that had been prophesied for several hundred years before that; it was written in the ancient Scriptures; it was even foretold of the signs that would happen at the birth of the messiah that would usher in a new age — because the expectancy had been built up through generation after generation, especially among the Essenes — when the angel announced himself unto Mary and spoke unto her that she would conceive a son, that she would bear the son who would be the messiah, and that his name would be Jeshua, meaning "The Lord is salvation" — the realization of the Lord is salvation — she understood what this meant and she was willing, for her next words were, "Be it done unto me according to the will of our Heavenly Father." And she knew that she would conceive and bear a son, the messiah. She didn't stand and protest and say, "Oh, no. I don't believe in miracles. It can't happen." She didn't say that at all. Because the belief was so strong and the expectancy was so strong, it was done according to the belief.

So in what you would call the fullness of time, my body, the physical vehicle that I expressed with during that lifetime, was born. You have read in your Holy Scriptures the story of how my father, Joseph, and my mother, Mary, were asked — not that they felt they had a choice — but they were asked to go unto Bethlehem to be counted for the census. And it came at a time when others would see this as being inopportune, in that my mother was very large with child. It was not a comfortable time for her to be traveling.

My father, Joseph, my earthly father — who was as a father to me and as a beloved brother — when he learned that Mary was with child, he was hesistant to take her as wife, for he knew that he had not lain with her and he did not know if anyone else had. He knew that she said an angel had appeared unto her, and he believed that this could be. But he was aware of the world thinking and he questioned what would others say if he took unto himself a wife who was already with child. And it gave him hesitation. It gave him a chance to look at what his beliefs were and what was important for him.

He had been chosen by the Brotherhood — seen and unseen — to be my earthly father. He was chosen....

Joseph

I was chosen because of my training, because of my gentleness, my strength and my courage, and it was felt that I would be a good earthly father unto the one known as Jeshua. Some years before, an angel had appeared to Enos, then head of the Essenes, and told him that I should be the one to be as father unto Jeshua, and Enos, before he laid down the body, passed the revelation on to the Elders of the Essenes at Mount Carmel.

As Jeshua has just said, I had my moments of hesitation. I had my moments of anguish. I had my moments of questioning whether I could fulfill the role and was this truly what Mary said that it was and what others said that it was going to be? And I ran and I hid and I wrestled with what I felt to be important.

Part of my wrestling was with my feeling of "what would others think?" How would my brothers, the monks, look upon me if I took a wife who was already with child? What would my family say? Yes, I thought about that.

And the one known as Judith gave me counsel and listened to my agonizing, and helped me see a larger vision. She helped calm my fears and to see that this was why I had come unto the earth plane at that time. I had often comforted her in her moments of doubt and agony as she was growing up, and she was able to share with me the peace and calm that I needed at that time.

So I took Mary to be my wife, and she was already with child and already, as you would say, with the fullness of the body, and we went unto Nazareth, my home village, where I began the carpentry business for which I am so famous.

There were many things that I did in that lifetime and carpentry was one of them. Healing was another. For I had what was called the gift of healing, and I healed many of my brothers and sisters. But carpentry is the one that has been so noted in your Scriptures.

We had been in Nazareth a short time when it was announced that there would be a census taken, that everyone needed to travel unto the city of their ancestors' birth, the lineage, as it would be. And being of the house of David, it meant that we would go unto Bethlehem to be counted. It was ordered for everyone to go unto the city of his ancestors, of his family, to be recorded as to name and age, profession or what you did for a living, what you owned, so that you could be taxed — and also what religious persuasion, so that you could be categorized.

And so Mary and I set out for Bethlehem. Mary was very much with child. Her time was quite near and it was not a journey that a woman would want to make at that time — for those of you who have had children know that when you get to be near the time of giving birth, it is like moving two bodies around — which, of course, it is — and it is like steering a large vehicle.

18

Jeshua

Within the Essene brotherhood my birth had been foretold and the Essene community knew that Mary's child was to be the messiah. But the Essenes also knew that this was not information that should be commonly shared with the Romans or with Herod, who was the overseerer of the territory. The Romans and Herod, in particular, would not want to see another ruler, as they would see it, a ruler upon this plane. It would be seen as a threat.

The Essenes knew that my birth needed to be kept quiet. And because there was a network that had been established long ago, there was an Essene in Bethlehem who ran an inn. He was the head of the Essenes in Bethlehem. And to the Romans and to the other Jews, he was nothing more than an innkeeper who was very much focused upon running the inn and supplying ones with food and wine and lodging. And yet, this one was very learned. He had a keen mind and a loving heart and was a true servant of the Heavenly Father.

So when it was known that my mother, Mary, and father, Joseph, would be making the trek to Bethlehem to be counted, word was sent out in advance unto this one to prepare a place for my mother. And it was not felt that to come unto the inn that was full of all of the ones who were there to be counted, yes, but there to have a good time as well, that this would be a suitable place for Mary to come and for the messiah to be born.

When they arrived, my father went into the inn and requested a place. Mary was with him at his side and her time had come. The innkeeper, knowing that the inn — a tavern with lodging you would call it — was not the place to have one such as Mary, said at first that there was no room in the inn — for he wanted to keep up the appearance of being the innkeeper. He knew and Joseph knew and Mary knew that there would be room, but it would not be in the inn.

Upon further questioning, very reluctantly the innkeeper said, "There are some caves to the back that I use as stables. You may go and spend the night there, if you so wish." And Joseph knew that this was the place for them.

Now, these were caves that were quite dry, quite comfortable, and even though they were used as stables for the animals, they were clean. It fulfilled the Scriptures that said that I would be born in a manger, that I would be born in a lowly place — humble, yes, and yet it was not what you would see as uncomfortable. It was quite warm and very comforting, and the animals were there at my birth and they knew themselves to be one with the Light that I am and that all are.

Mary's time was fulfilled that evening and I was born, welcomed into the world by a midwife and several Essene women who helped with the birth, as well. Joseph was sent to the entrance of the cave to watch and to abide within his heart, for he was being as many men are who are going to be fathers: he was being very nervous and very much wanting to help, to assuage the pain that he felt Mary was enduring — and yet Mary bore it all with equanimity.

There is an intensity accompanying a birth — as is true not only on the physical level, but upon the level of a birth of a new perception, a change in your way of thinking, a change in the way that you love. Oftentimes changes are born with great intensity. And as you are going through the birth process, there can be much anguish, much feeling of being pushed, perhaps against the will and yet, there is an energy that is pushing you into a new birth, a new way of expressing. And it can be painful.

There was a great light in the heavens: the Star that had been foretold. It was caused by the conjunction of several planets. Astrologers had seen this from afar off: ones who were studying the ancient prophecies and knew this would be a sign of the birth of the messiah at this time. I emphasize "at this time" for, with the birth of each age, there is a birth of a messiah, and this was not the first time that I, as the Christ — not I as Jeshua, but I as the Christ — was born upon this plane.

Each time the prophecies have spoken of various signs to be seen in the heavens and this was true at my birth, as well. There were signs of the stars, the planets coming into conjunction with each other that made such a light that it was seen by all upon the known world at that time.

This is why the ones known as the Wise Men traveled from afar, for they had seen the movement in the heavens and they knew this to be a sign of the birth of one who was to be a great leader. And so they traveled.

The star that was seen has meaning on many levels. It was, as the astrologers saw, a conjuction of planets reflecting the light back to the Earth, reflecting the Light that you are to this Earth. Ones have said that it was a great starship that came to witness the birth. And this is true, as well, for there were many of your brothers and sisters expressing in a different realm, dimension, who were here as well, for they had felt the acceleration of the energy that would bring forth the demonstration upon this plane at that time. They also have their historians, as you would call them, the ones who study the mystical writings. They also have their inner wisdom. And they came to witness this in what you would call your starships, and they were seen by ones who had the eyes to see, and by others they were not seen.

The light of the star symbolizes the Light not only of my birth, but the Light that you are, the Light that mankind in this age has been willing to accept and to acknowledge as himself/herself. For there are those of you who have always been in oneness in the awareness, in oneness with the Light that you are, and there were many who felt the energy that was brought together by what was symbolized by my birth.

It was not just my birth that was important. It was the coming together of the conscousness, of readiness, of willingness to accept the Light, your divine inheritance of being the Child of the Heavenly Father. There was a readiness upon this plane, an expectancy — as there is **now**, in this day and time. It is not an expectancy in this day and time of a birth of a messiah as one individual, coming to be the saviour of the world that will change everything in the world — although there are still those who look to another to save them — but there is a growing expectancy of awareness of Who you are, an acceleration of occurances that are bringing it right in front of the face of everyone who is willing to look at it and to say that there must be more to living. "There must be more to life than just what this body would speak to me, of what these eyes would show me and what the ears would tell me. There is a longing in my heart to come Home." And this is felt by many of your brothers and sisters. There is a birthing that is happening upon this plane, again.

The three Wise Men, as they have been called, were mystics, scholars, astrologers — ones who studied the heavenly bodies and knew the symbolism of not only what was happening in the configuration of the heavenly bodies, but knew what this meant according to the prophecies. And they were ones... there were actually five in number.

There were three who came initially. These three are the ones who went unto Herod and asked him where the new king was to be born, for they had seen the signs in the heavens. This was news to him, and Herod very much wanted to know where this new king was going to be born for he did not want a threat to his rulership. And so he said unto them he did not know but when they found out, would they please come and tell him, for he wanted to go and worship the new king. He did not want to go and worship, but he wanted to know the whereabouts of this new king.

Those three were led unto Bethlehem by the signs, the star, the conjunction of the planets in the heavens.

When they arrived in Bethlehem, they did not come to see me immediately. Some time passed. Mary and Joseph stayed in the cave behind the inn for forty days after my birth. This was to allow Mary time to gain her strength. This also allowed time for everyone to disperse, to go back to their homes, everyone who had come to be counted, and also for the news of the star — for everyone had seen the star that night and all had interpreted it in their own way, but all knew that it was of special signifcance — to decrease in attention. It was not thought to be advantageous to allow everyone to know that there had been a babe born on that night under that star, for many would interpret it with fear.

And so Mary and Joseph made their home in the stable for some forty days, and it was at the end of this time that the three Wise Men came, joined by two more who had traveled from what is known as Persia and from India, who had also seen the signs in the heavens and knew this to be the fulfillment of the prophecy regarding the birth of a messiah. Thus, the three Wise Men — as it is recorded in your Scriptures — were actually five, and they came to visit me. They wanted to see what God Himself would look like — and yet, if you will receive it, all you have to do is to look upon your sister or upon your brother or in the mirror and you see the face of God.

But they came to behold the new King of Kings and to see what manner of parents had been chosen as worthy to usher in this birth. And at first they were surprised by what they saw. For Joseph was simple of manner, great of heart, but seemed to be, to these learned men, just a simple carpenter. And Mary seemed to be a little Hebrew mother, and yet there was a beauty, a purity, a love that was felt in her presence.

So when they appeared at the entrance of the cave and Joseph came to meet them, they at first looked, as the world would look, upon appearances. And they were ushered into the cave and Mary, being the hostess, served them sweets and some wine to drink, being hospitable. And she poured for herself a goblet of wine, as well, and joined them at table. And the Wise Men, coming from different cultures, were surprised at this. For in their cultures women did not assume equality. Women would serve and remain in the background. But Mary, being of the Essene community, was very much the equal of any man and they soon found this to be true as they engaged Joseph and Mary in conversation.

At first the conversation was a bit awkward and strained, for the Wise Men did not know what they could talk about with ones seemingly so simple. So Joseph led the conversation around to the star that had appeared in the heavens the night of my birth and the Wise Men talked of the signs in the heavens and, as they did this, the interchange enlivened. And they talked of numerology and they talked of mystical symbolism and they talked of the ancient writings and they talked of the spaceships, the starships.

And the Wise Men saw that these were no simple peasants, that truly they were the servants of the Heavenly Father, well versed in the ancient writings.

And then, they wished to see me, and Mary led them to the manger, which surprised them, for having been called the King of Kings, they did not expect to see me lying in a manger with a bed of straw. But I will share with you that it was a very comfortable bed. I wanted for nothing. There were plenty of woolen blankets. There was the straw. Yes, there were the sheep and the oxen and the goat, and we had conversations, the animals and I. For we are one. The Life force is one.

And as they approached the manger with all these questions in their mind, again coming from the perspective of appearances, the place of the world, Mary picked me up and cradled me in her arm to bring me over to them — and they beheld the Light that they are. They thought it was the Light around me — which was true. They thought it was the Light around Mary — which was true. But what they saw was a mirror of the Light that they are, and they fell down in awe because of their belief, their expectancy that the King of Kings, the Messiah, would be so great. And yet, when they lifted up their eyes, Mary said, "Look, he is but a babe, just as you have been."

And the three Wise Men — otherwise known as five — remembered even more wisdom in that evening.

There were the gifts that were given unto me: the gold, the frankincense and the myrrh — all spiritual gifts in tangible form. The gold symbolized the purity of the Light that I am — and that you are. The golden coins are the golden white Light of Energy in tangible form that allows an exchange on the Earth plane. For truly, when Mary and Joseph needed to go unto Egypt when I was very small, some of the gold was used to make the journey and to provide for their stay in Egypt. Later on, when I was eighteen, I used some of it to travel unto India to study with the masters there.

Always in that lifetime, whatever was needed was provided for me — as it is for you. There are times when you may feel that the golden coins are a bit slow in coming and that it is much easier to be in the flow of giving them out than it is to be in the receiving of them, and perhaps the receiving doesn't come quite as fast as you feel the flow is going out —

this is the way of the world — but always the golden coins are there for you. Whether it is the golden coins or it is the piece of plastic, it matters not. It is the energy. It is the energy of your consciousness, Who you are, being supposedly manifested without you and yet, the source is within you. You will always have enough golden coins — as I did.

The frankincense is a resin from a tree that grew in Persia and was presented unto me by the Wise Man, the learned one from Persia. It was a gift of value and it was a gift of signifcance in its symbolism. For as the incense is burned, what is seen is a connection from this plane unto another realm. As you see the smoke of the incense rising, it symbolizes for you the coming from this plane and rising unto what you would see as another plane above you. It is not truly that any plane is above you — it is within you — but it has the symbolism of reminding you of your ascending spiritual nature.

The myrrh is also a resin, from a tree that grew in India. It also had great value and great significance. It has been said that it symbolized the bitterness of life upon this plane, for if it is tasted, it has a bitter flavor. But there was more in that time that it symbolized: it was used for healing and it symbolized healing. It symbolized the wholeness of the body, the wholeness of the body as an expression of the Light and the Love that you are.

You see, there is always a deeper significance, and the Wise Men knew the symbolism. The gifts that were given were of the utmost symbolism and the highest in regard at that time by the ones who studied the ancient writings, the ones who were of what you would call the mystery schools. This was the highest respect, reverence, honor that could be paid unto one. They were gifts that would be given unto a king, and they were presented unto me as a way of honoring, a way of acknowledging.

And yet, if you will receive it, they are gifts that are given unto you as well. For what has happened in what you would see as my lifetime and my birth is your story as well. For you are the Christ Child being birthed upon this plane. And it is truly a birth to be celebrated — for I know what is to be. And what a grand celebration it is.

You will go as the Light that you are, unimpeded by the constrictions that you have for lifetimes accepted, unimpeded by a feeling of unworthiness, unimpeded by the voice of separation. You will go with such freedom and such spontaneity, for you will be in the very flow of the Light that you are, and there will be seen such beauty upon this plane that has not been seen for what you would call eons of time. It is truly an age of celebration, and the time comes rapidly now.

In this time of your holidays the world would speak unto you of celebrating the birth of one Jeshua ben Joseph, who was born, as you would see it, almost two thousand years ago, the birth of one who was very God upon this plane and who has ascended unto the right hand of God and sits there, according to some belief systems, in judgment upon his brothers and sisters. **Never** do I sit in judgment upon anyone, for I know Who I am and I know Who you are, and I know that you are the beloved Child of our Heavenly Father, the same as I am.

In this time of your holidays celebrate with great joy. Give the gifts, as is your custom, but know always that the gift of the heart, the love that accompanies any physical object that is given, the love is truly the gift. The object, as you have seen, in time will crumble unto dust, but the love remains eternally.

Go with a simplicity this year in your holidays. Approach all of the activities with a simplicity, for truly, beloved one, in another hundred years will it be remembered whether you had a six-foot Christmas tree or a three-foot one?

Truly, it will not. But the Love within the heart is what abides forever. Nurture in every moment the Love that you are. See and behold the Light that your brothers and sisters are. See the very Light around them as you behold their countenance. Do this even in physical form: to look upon one and to diffuse the focus of the eyes just enough to be able to take in the Light that is termed the aura. Feel yourself to be one with the very vibration of the one who is in front of you. Know that your energy intermingles with everyone's energy. With the one who sits next to you, you are exchanging energy at all times. And, if you would receive it, you are breathing in the very air that this one has just expelled, and vice versa. Even on the physical level there is much exchange, interchange.

In this time of your holidays, pause in each moment and make it holy by remembering that you are the holy one. You are the Child whose birth is being celebrated. It is not to merely celebrate the birth of one

Jeshua ben Joseph: One who came and expressed upon this plane, just as you are. One who found himself to be utilizing a male body, who had the very human feelings of doubt, of unworthiness from time to time, of questions. One who studied the ancient Scriptures. One who read all of the prophecies. One who heard all of the stories about his birth and who wondered if he could ever grow into the shoes, the sandals, that the messiah was supposed to wear. One who felt sorrow when others who were loved laid down the body, and who felt parted from their physical company until he remembered that there is no parting, that the communion always exists, but that the constictions of limited awareness must be gently released. One who felt great love for his brothers and sisters. One who felt physical attraction unto a beauteous one who came as a helpmate.

I experienced all of the feelings of a man upon this plane. For what would it serve if I came to be a teacher, a counselor, a brother, if I did not know all of the feelings and emotions that you experience from time to time? I also experienced the emotions so that I knew how to take that feeling of emotion and to look at it in another way, to shift the perception and to see it in the largest view — not just the view of the world that would speak of constriction and of suffering and of sorrow, of loss, of pain — but to be able to see it in the flow of eternity and to say that Love is Who I am. I and the Father are one. You and the Father are one.

If you exist — and I assure you that you do — you are very Life upon this plane. You are the Life of the Heavenly Father expressing moment by moment upon this plane, and you need do nothing more than to just be Who you are: to be the Love that you are. To sit with a child and to share with a child and to say, "I love you." To share with a flower, to share with a beloved pet, to share with a co-worker, the Love that they are. To say to one who is hurrying about, "Stop. Pause for a moment. You know, I love you." It will change their perception of the world and it will greatly enhance the wisdom of the Wise Men. All of you are very Life upon this plane. All of you are expressing the various talents, abilities that you feel yourself to have in this focus. You have all talents and you have all abilties. You are unlimited. You are infinite in expression, but there is a focus that you have chosen in what you would see as this lifetime. Share those abilities and talents freely and they will grow.

Go with joyousness in this holiday season, for that is truly what this season is for. You manifest this holiday season every year. Would there be a reason? I share with you that there is a reason: it is to bring up for yourself at least once a year the opportunity of seeing your holiness, of pausing for a moment in this season of joy and knowing you are that joy. Where can that joy come from? It does not come from a greeting card. It is not manufactured by your company known as Hallmark. You are that very joy itself as you accept and allow the Love that you are to stream forth in freedom. You are the Child of our Heavenly Father. You are blessed.

You are everything that has been ascribed unto me. Think upon that in your moments when you would judge what you have done or thought or said and times when you may have felt that you were not quite good enough or you haven't done whatever — and the list goes on and on.

You are everything that has been ascribed unto me. You are the great ray of Light forever ongoing, forever expressing. It matters not what a brother or sister would choose to express unto you in one moment, for truly you live in eternity. The Love that you are is whole, lacking for nothing. It does not need to come to you from the outside from another one. Others will make their choices and they will go upon their journey. And you bless them for their choices, for you know that in time the One that I have called the Grand Weaver will take all of the threads of the various choices and weave them together into a beautiful tapestry that brings the sleeping Child of our Heavenly Father back to wakefulness.

So even though you would see them as making the choices that are the detours — and yet, that is a judgment — even though you would see them as making the choices that would seem to be the detours, know that that is their journey Home. It is something that they have chosen to experience and there will be blessings upon that path, as well, for them. And if they choose to spend it with you, there is much joy. If they choose not to spend it with you, there is much joy.

All of you have manifested for yourself what would seem to be the individualities of brothers and sisters upon this plane, ones that you would see expressing with the different bodily forms, and yet they are as mirrors for you. For you would look upon one and see an action and judge it to be hurtful, constricting. Another would look upon the action and just say, "Well, a porcupine just has the nature to be a porcupine."

All of you in this time, in what you call your holidays, are manifesting for yourselves a grand opportunity to choose: either to choose for the world and the activities that would tell you to rush hither and thither, to go here and to buy this and, "Is this gift good enough? Should I buy another?" Always choices. But it is a grand opportunity to say, "Where do I abide? What is my true nature? Who am I?" And to pause and to come unto the place of power: not as the world defines power, but that place of power which is the Love and the peace of the heart.

Especially in this time you give unto yourselves a grand choice, for the world speaks loudly in the weeks before what you would see as a holy time. And it is truly a holy time, for it gives unto you a grand opportunity, a time of wholing.

Pause in each moment to know your own holiness. It is not a time to celebrate my birth as the world would speak unto you, to speak of a birth that happened two thousand years ago, the birth of one Jeshua ben Joseph, who was very God upon this plane — and I was and I am and you are — but it is to pause and to celebrate your own birth. And what comes quickly now for you is the awareness that you are as I am.

You are my sister, expressing in this time and in this place. You are my brother, the Child of our Heavenly Father — as I am — and you have chosen to express in this time and space the Love that you are, as it was seen that I came and expressed the Love that I am, to make a demonstration as it would be. And yet, what I did you do also. You have done in physical form what has been ascribed unto me.

For how would you relate unto what happened, the circumstances of my life? How would you understand? How would you feel an alignment in the heart with the very events that are ascribed unto me in that lifetime? How would you know that if you had not experienced it, as you would see it, some time, some where, some space? A thought to ponder. For you cannot relate to something that you have not experienced on some, as you would see, level. Food for thought.

You also are experiencing upon this plane all of the challenges and all of the joys that have been ascribed unto that lifetime for me as you meet with your brothers and sisters and they bring up for you something to look at right in front of the face, a challenge. Each day brings its gifts. Each day brings unto you the choice of, "Where do I abide?" And you are choosing more rapidly to abide in the place of the heart. A wise choice.

Beloved one, you are of a lineage that goes back farther than time, farther than you would see time. For truly you are the only Child of our Heavenly Father. And as you would see time evolving upon this plane, there has been a certain lineage of ones who have been in alignment with what has been called the mystical writings, the mystical teachings, the ancient knowledge.

You are now at a place of saying, "I wish to know Who I am." Have you not said that? Yes. All of you have said that from time to time. "Who am I? Why am I here?" And you have called out from the very depths of your soul to experience — not just to know it with the mind, not just to know it in a book, not just to have someone come and tell you — but "I want to know."

"I want to live it." And when the soul decides to experience the holiness that you are, all of creation rearranges itself to facilitate your desire. And that is what you are experiencing now in this time, as you would see it, these closing years of what you would see as this decade and this century and this millennium. It is truly an exciting time to be alive, and that is why you have chosen to be here. You are all grand adventurers. Some of you would say, "Who? Me?" and yet it is true. You would not be expressing with the body upon this plane at this time if you were not grand adventurers. For it is a grand time to be alive, as you would see it, with the molecules of physicality, to have the body to express with.

The Christmas Story is your story. This year in your holidays is the celebration of your birth. This is why I spoke unto you earlier to pause in each moment and to ask, "Is this the voice of the world that would ask me to run hither and thither and to meet all of these deadlines?" And truly when you are caught up in the deadlines, it is deadly, for you are forgetting Who you are. This year celebrate your own birth as the Christ Child that you are.

You have asked to know Who you are, and you are creating the consciousness that will make the Remembrance possible. It is not that I and my brothers, ones you would see as great masters, are going to come and present for you, in front of you, something that is already accomplished. For you, as the master that you are, have free choice always to accept it now or to say, "No, I will pass." And you have said that in many lifetimes: "No, not yet. Later on I'll get around to that. Let me experience one more drama of suffering, one more drama of constriction." And you have put it off another year or another lifetime.

But I will share with you, if you will receive it, that you have chosen to accept your holiness. You will this year accept at least some measure of knowing the Light that you are and the power of the Light that you are. And it will grow. As you have the willingness to open the heart to yourself and to your brothers and sisters, the Love that you are rushes forth and is expressed. And as it rushes forth, you know yourself to be that Love.

Love is not something that you can go and purchase at the specialty store. It is not something that you can go to your grand malls and shop for — although the shopping is fun. I love to abide in your malls and to watch you and your brothers and sisters. Many of your brothers and sisters rush about tightly wrapped up in the energy that they are, not knowing the joy that even such a little thing as buying a gift for another can be.

When you give unto another something that you would express your love with, there is an openness, a physical opening that happens with the energy of the heart chakra, as it would be called, and it opens and the Love and the Light that you are pours forth. It can be measured even by your scientists with the technology that you now have. It can be seen.

As you behold a beloved friend, a pet, a flower, something of beauty, and you become one with that one — the beloved friend, the pet, the child, the flower in its unfoldment — you open the shutters of the heart and allow the energy that you are to pour forth in its radiance.

So you can imagine as you and as your brothers and sisters go rushing about in the malls trying to select the right gift and feeling so constricted about it, what does this do to the very energy that you are? It closes it down. And it doesn't even feel good, does it?

I, too, experienced the emotions that you are experiencing and, as you would see, growing through. I, too, experienced the constrictions. I, too, experienced the frustrations, the self-doubts within myself. But as I allowed myself to return to the peace of the heart, there was also the Voice within me that told me what I knew to be true, told me that I was more than the emotion I was feeling. For truly you are not the emotion. It is something that you experience. And you can abide with it for a lifetime — many lifetimes — and many lifetimes you have stayed with the experience of a predominant emotion until you have come to a place where the soul has said, "Enough, already. I want to experience something else," and then you have chosen anew.

The beauty that you behold in the flower that is opening before you is there in its process for you as you. You are its creator and you are one with the very energy that is unfolding before you. And it is symbolizing for you the unfoldment that is taking place within your consciousness.

So as you look upon your flowers at this time of your holidays, and you watch them as they are growing and they are opening for you and sharing with you their beauty and their process, it is showing you what is happening with you, as well. Many of your brothers and sisters pass by the flower and do not even see it. They do not even know that the beauty is there, that there is Life in that form, pouring forth its beauty for you, its love for you. And yet, those of you who pause and abide in the heart can drink in the very beauty of the tiniest alpine flower or the largest tropical flower. They are all there for you, as Christmas gifts — even in July — if you have the eyes to see it.

Many of your brothers and sisters will go rushing through this season to celebrate my birth, thinking it to be something that happened a long time ago and that I am far off, away, and that I need to be worshipped. I do not want your worship. I want your friendship, the equality of brothers. I want you to come Home with me.

This Christmas season, this Christmas day, give yourself a Christmas gift. Ask of yourself, "What gift would I like this Christmas?" And after you have considered all the tangible gifts you might desire, abide within the stillness of your own heart and ask, "What gift is most important? If I could have any gift, what would I ask for?" Would it be the gift of peace, of love, of gentleness, of companionship, healing, abundance, unlimitedness? Would you give yourself permission to love yourself, to play with the joy of the Child within, to take time for yourself, to rest and abide in the heart? For truly all healing and all wisdom come from the

Heart. Would you gift yourself the Remembrance of Who you are?

Pause for a moment, right now, and know the Heart that you are.

It is not that I, as some great master, can come and grant unto you the wishes, but because you have come unto a place of clarity within the heart and you have asked that these gifts be made manifest for you, your desires will be made manifest. You have come unto a place of awareness, in consciousness, of saying, "This is what is important for me." And with that very step you have set into motion the manifestation of what you have asked for. It remains only now for you to accept what you have asked for, for these gifts are truly yours already. This is why we have spoken unto you that this is your holiday season. These are your holy days. You are the one who is making it holy by the fact that you are holy. When you awaken on Christmas morning, say unto yourself, "This is my birthday. Happy birthday," and share it with the one known as Jeshua ben Joseph. Know that it is the birth of the Christ Child that you are.

This Christmas season, this Christmas day, give unto yourself the gift of Christmas. Do not celebrate someone's birth that happened a long time ago, but celebrate the birth of your Self. When you awaken on that morning, when the eyes first pop open, say unto yourself, "This is my birthday," and know that all of the gifts that are given are given unto you.

This is a truth, for what you see in your world and what you see in front of you is what you are manifesting in your consciousness. Others of your brothers and sisters will manifest other events and activities on Christmas day. Those will be their gifts, whether of loving form or not. But for yourself on Christmas day, when you first awaken, say unto yourself, "This is my birthday. This is the day I celebrate the birth of the Christ Child that I am." And invite me to be one with you and I will be, for I love a celebration.

Know that I walk always with you. If I, as the one known as Jeshua ben Joseph, if I can love you — and I do — know yourself to be worthy. I know Who you are. The world does not. I know Who you are and you are beautiful. You are worthy. You are Love itself. This Christmas season, accept the Love that you are.

Beloved one, you have answered an invitation, an invitation for Remembrance of the One that we are. This season, these holidays, are a celebration of your birth. What are you going to do with these holidays?

Will you celebrate with me the birth of the one Christ Child?

The Love that you are streams forth in such effulgence that if you could behold yourself, beloved one, the way I see you, you would never doubt your worthiness again. You are the beautiful radiance of the Heavenly Father Himself. Go with the joy that is your inheritance. You are the Child of the Beloved One.

So be it.

Questions and Answers:

What does the name "Jeshua ben Joseph" mean?

"Jeshua" was the name given by the angel unto my mother, Mary, to be my name in that incarnation, and it means "The Lord is salvation." When you remember the Lord your God in holiness, in wholeness, in one-ness, and acknowledge within the depth of what you would call your soul that you are one with the Heavenly Father, that is your salvation, that is your remembrance of the Light that you are, and you are no longer constricted by the beliefs of the world that would speak to you of separation and all that comes from the soil thereof.

Ben means "of" and "Joseph" was my father. This was the way in that culture of identifying sons and daughters of fathers. For my sister Ruth was known as Ruth ben Joseph. Do you see? That is what "Jeshua ben Joseph" means: "Jeshua, the son of Joseph". It was written YSHW, and more correctly pronounced, "Yeshwa". "Jesus" is the Greek form of my name.

You had brothers and sisters, right?

Yes.

So genetically, were they your half brothers and sisters? Yours was a miracle birth, but your brothers and sisters, genetically were they exactly like you?

Every birth upon this plane is a miracle, and yet it is the natural development of a process that has been set in motion with a desire and an agreement. Upon the physical plane in expression my brothers and sisters were what you would see as a combining, a coming together of the genes of Joseph and of Mary, so that technically in the way the world would see this they were my half brothers and half sisters in that they shared the genes of Joseph.

I came as a thought process — as they did also — but I took only the molecules of physicality from the body of the one who was chosen to be my mother, from Mary, sharing of what would be seen on a physical level as her genes, bringing together from those physical molecules, making it into what you would see as the body that was birthed. It was a marriage that happened, in that it was the Thought, with a capital "T", a divine Thought — not just a thought that would be fleeting in the world like, "This might be a good idea." Not that kind of thought at all, but the Thought that manifests. It was the coming together of the

Thought and the willingness of the belief of Mary to manifest a body through her: to be, as you would see it, a hostess for a time being for the body that was birthed through her.

So, yes, as the world would view it, my brothers and sisters, because they were sharing of the genes, the physical molecules of Joseph, and of the thought process, the consciousness of Joseph coming together with Mary, they would be seen technically as my half brothes and sisters. And yet, I would ask you, how can anyone be a half? One is always a whole.

And did you have red hair?

Yes. It was what you would call auburn, sort of a golden red. Yes, there were many tones of red in it.

Were you actually born in August or December?

In late summer.

Well, why is it in December that we celebrate it?

This was for the purpose of bringing together celebrations that already were being celebrated at this time of year, the time when the light seen in what you would call the Northern hemisphere upon this physical plane is at its lowest. There were many celebrations throughout what you would see as history that have occurred at this time because you would remind yourself of the Light that you are. When you would see upon the Holy Mother, the Earth, a time of more darkness than of the light, when the days are shorter, it was your way of remembering in an outward ceremony the Light that you are. And this was celebrated in many civilizations as a way of remembering Who you are.

Even in this time, there are cultures that have what you would not call a Christmas celebration, but would have a celebration of lights, which comes at this very time of year. And so it was thought by the ones in your religious organization, which was very strong at that time, making many decisions for the brothers and sisters upon this plane, that it would be a good idea to make the Christian celebration — as they have termed it — come at the same time as some of the pagan — as they called it — celebrations.

That is why Christmas, the celebration of my birth, comes at this time, and it is a good remembrance. At a time when you would see the light upon the physical plane growing darker, coming to a diminishment and then again expanding into the light that you see by midsummer, the celebration is a good remembrance of the Light that you are. It is not by accident that this comes as a celebration at this time.

If it were not the celebration of my birth, which was put there by your religious fathers — who are not your fathers at all; they are your brothers — if it were not the celebration of my birth, then there would be another celebration to remind you of the Light that you are.

I have a question regarding the three Wise Men — or the five.

{Laughter.}

Yes, the five known as three.

Certain groups have claimed that the three Wise Men were certain people.

Yes, and this has been true down through the ages. At this point of focus, this time and space, there is a belief that these were ones known as ascended masters who have come back now to teach in this time, to share with the brothers and sisters a knowledge and a wisdom, a remembrance, if you will. And this is well and good for those who would accept that belief. For there are various languages that are spoken, and all is for the point of being the catalyst for remembrance. And for those that this belief is shared with, if it sparks the remembrance of Who they are, then this has served its mission.

It is not important for everyone to identify the energies as being certain individuals. You have heard it said that the Wise Men were certain ascended masters with whom your culture is acquainted in this day and time, and for those who understand that language and that language has value and meaning for them, then it is a step on the way to remembrance. But for others these names would mean nothing. The very vibrations would go by and elicit no understanding, no relatedness. There would be other identities that would speak unto them, and they would put the identities upon that personage and it would have value for them. It is like, as you would see, my incarnations known by different names, different individuals in different times, and yet the energy is the Christ energy.

The energy that was being shown forth through the Wise Men, be it three or five, be it known by individual names, was the energy of the Christ — ones who were in tune with the mystical Oneness, who had studied and knew themselves to be one — not only through that lifetime but through many other lifetimes which brought them unto that point of expression.

And yes, for ones that it would have value, they may identify the three Wise Men as certain identifiable masters. Others would attach other names and other qualities to them. And yet, what has happened was that ones were willing to come in bodily form, to take on the molecules of physicality, to extend what needed to be extended and expressed at that time.

I would share with you that the two who came from what you would see as far countries manifested their bodies and the camels on which they rode at a certain point in time, and when the service was ended, they again allowed the energy to go back into what you would see as the cosmic forces.

But that is no different than what you do. You would see, perhaps, your time interval of a lifetime being from point zero to point seventy-eight, ninety-eight, sixty-five — whatever; pick a number — you would see that as a lifetime. Others manifest a body, looking perhaps to be thirty-five or so, and they will stay for what you would see as a period of months and then, when the purpose of having the body has been fulfilled, instantly they let the body disintegrate into the dust that it is. You would see that as a miracle, and yet what you are doing is as much a miracle. It is only the time frame that varies.

You see, when you approach a question such as you have asked, it needs to be seen against the backdrop of the tapestry of the Dream. The holy Child of our Father abides always within the Kingdom. All adventures are ones that have been in the Dream. They have been manifested through what you would call imagination, imaging. What you are doing, what I am doing right now is imaging: putting into what you would call physical form an image. So when you come unto a question such as this, see it against the backdrop of eternity and see it as being a truth — not the Truth because the Truth is you have never left the Kingdom. You have never gone upon all of the adventures that mankind thinks he/she has gone upon. These have been as dreams — some as nightmares. These have been as dreams.

So, yes, unto ones who would claim it to be a truth that the three Wise Men were certain individuated masters, it is a truth. The Truth is: you are the Holy Child of our

Father. You are a great ray of Light. You are Light. You are Love expressing eternally, unlimited, expressing in many forms in many fashions, but always the Light and Love that you were created to be before time was.

The other two that have never been talked about, was that because they only manifested for just a very short time and were gone again? Why do they remain mysteries when the three are touted so loudly?

The three are touted so highly because they were the ones who appeared unto Herod and they are the ones who are recorded in the Scriptures.

It was known that there were Wise Men who came and visited me as an infant — as *I* was an infant; they weren't — and this was what was recorded: the three who visited Herod. It was also recorded that the Wise Men came from afar. These were the two who traveled from afar. So, you see, it is a bringing together, a juxtaposition of facts you would call them, different stories being made into one, whereas actually there are various parts.

Did all five give you gifts? There are only three gifts recorded.

The three who appeared unto Herod were the ones who gave unto me the gold. The one from Persia gave unto me the frankincense, and the one who was from Indus gifted me the myrrh.

There is much, as you have seen, that appears on different levels. It is all a truth, as is the story of my birth that will be celebrated in your holidays. It is a truth for the purpose of bringing the Child Home again. This is its only purpose.

If it serves the purpose of awakening, well and good. Remember that all that transpires within this grand adventure is as a story. It is all a parable — as were the stories that I often told to the multitudes. It can be read on many levels. And for those who have eyes to see and ears to hear, there will be the insights. The in sights of inner wisdom.

Many religious sects talk about the Second Coming of Christ. Does that just mean it comes from the heart or is there going to be a physical coming? Has this question come to you before?

Never, beloved one. Never has this question been addressed before.

{Laughter.}

58

Truly it has — and this is the Christmas Story that is *your* story: the Second Coming of Christ.

And are there signs of the Second Coming that we will see, like the signs surrounding your birth?

I would ask you, beloved one, what is your knowing? Are there signs that are abounding in this world of yours, even at this time? Has anything come to mind? Has anything come right up in front of your face? You needn't answer right away. Ponder.

Yes. The signs, as you have termed them, are all around you. Have you felt an acceleration upon this plane, an acceleration of the holy Child wanting to know Who he/she is? Have you witnessed a growing awareness of oneness with our Holy Mother, the Earth, which is manifesting as a wave of interest in the ecology — a green awareness, I think it is called? Have you seen more of the brothers and sisters coming together in small groups, communities, to support and help each other? Even the ones that would be seen to be "acting out," as it is called, in violence are crying out, with grand intensity, to know Who they are. The signs, beloved one, are all around you.

There is a Second Coming of the Christ upon this plane, and it comes rapidly now. It is the birthing of the Remembrance of Who you truly are: the Christ incarnate, Love expressing in matter, physicality. It is the *second* coming in that you will *remember* your first coming upon our Holy Mother, the Earth.

So be it.

We have a vision.
It is a vision of Community.

The Community of Light

There is a new magic in the air, an energy of love and remembrance. The call to
awaken to our spiritual heritage is being
heard around the world and a planetary
reunion of heart families is in progress. We
welcome you in the spirit of brother/sister-
hood and invite you to share in our vision of
community.

The Community is to be a living demonstration to the world of how mankind,
through the one Mind and one Heart, can
live in harmony with Mother Earth and in
service to our Holy Father and fellow man.
We envision the Community as educational
in the broadest sense of the word, a place
where people can come to be nurtured by
the very Light of the Christ that we all are,
to celebrate that Light, to experience again
the love, joy, beauty, wisdom, harmony and
peace of the Heavenly Father and the Holy
Mother Earth. We are open to learning from
others and to sharing that which we know
to reach the place of remembrance in all.

Philosophy

We acknowledge the Christ presence in all and use our inner knowing and the sharings of teachers as guidelines for our own growth and understanding. We allow the true meaning of unconditional love to dictate our actions to further the cause of peace in the world, respect for all life, and the empowerment of each person to fulfill his/her highest potential. We acknowledge the union between body, mind, and spirit both within ourselves and with all life forms. We believe in the abundance of God and acknowledge that all limitations are held within our own mind. We are open to change as our awareness expands and new information unfolds.

Life-style

All peoples and life-styles are accepted with the understanding that we live in non-violence, respectful of others, and are committed to being honest with ourselves and others. We see all members supporting the vision and activities of the community and being accountable for the consequences of our thoughts and actions.

Maintaining a healthy body through nutrition, exercise and attitude is valued.

Each individual is free to choose the method that best suits his or her preferences. Classes and techniques for allowing the healing forces of the body to speak of its needs will be available.

The Community members are primarily vegetarians and all community meals will be vegetarian. Our vision is to provide the majority of our food from our own organically grown crops.

Creative free-time, spiritual play and laughter are necessary ingredients in our lifestyle, as are quiet times to commune with God within our own being and times of sharing. Opportunities will be available for the sharing of meals, classes, workshops, chapel services, and experiencing the glory of nature. A deep communion with the angelic, devic, elemental and animal kingdoms will be integral to community living.

Government

The Community is affiliated with Oakbridge University, an educational, religious and charitable non-profit corporation. The University Board of Directors handles the corporate business issues of the community. Within the community, each area of operation has a team of interested and knowledgeable persons who research information to bring to the community meetings. Decisions within the community are made by a consensus of all members. All projects and decisions support the purpose of the community.

Activities and Services

The Community intends to provide a school for young people with a curriculum based on the philosophy of the community. Through example, experience, and study, we will incorporate various learning styles in the teaching of spiritual principles, cooperation, personal growth, basic skills and application. We honor nature, creative expression, and inner knowing as major influences in our learning process.

Oakbridge University will offer classes and workshops at the Community in the areas of whole life healing, spirituality and personal growth. Our teachers are professionals from many areas of expertise and background. Our University is open to all and class costs are reasonable.

We encourage our members to be open to continuous growth and the sharing of information. A library will be incorporated within the vision of the Community Center to facilitate and inspire. In addition, we envision a bookstore/ resource center where a broad range of materials and topics will be available for purchase and/or rental.

The Community is a healing community. Our primary vision is the wholeness of each person on the planet, activated through the remembrance of who we are. This will bring about health of body, mind and spirit, and the unlimited joy this healing brings. Many methods of healing will be available at the Community as well as classes on the various techniques which facilitate healing.

Since the Community is committed to helping individuals in the areas of health and vitality, and to preserving the environment, our health food center will offer a wide variety of nutritional products and environmentally-safe organic home products.

Our plan also includes a vegetarian restaurant and bakery that will be open to the public.

A Sustainable Way Of Life

In an environment of acceptance and creativity, each member is encouraged to use intuition and guidance in the creation of an energy-efficient, functional, attractive community that serves the resident members and visitors.

Community living areas and individual dwellings will be accented by gardens, wooded areas and play areas. All structures will exceed the standard for energy efficiency. Energy sources will be explored with the goal of making the community self-sufficient. Recycling and renewal of resources will be a part of all projects.

Traffic within the community proper will be minimal as most vehicles will be parked on the perimeter of the common grounds. Service vehicles will be used for deliveries. Bicycles and other non-polluting vehicles will be welcome.

Members

There is no membership fee to join our community. All prospective resident members must meet with the Admissions Committee before joining the Community to decide if the vision of the Community is in harmony with their own. New resident members are expected to support the community through participation and whatever financial or time commitments seem appropriate.

We who envision living in harmony with each other and the earth in a cooperative, synergistic environment have come together with a single purpose — to be that demonstration of how individuals joined together as one Heart and one Mind can serve the awakening of the whole of mankind, remembering always that we are one with God.

If you have felt a recognition and a harmony within yourself in reading about the Community and would like to support such a vision, please know that we welcome your participation and contribution.

Oakbridge University
A Washington Nonprofit Corporation
6716 Eastside Drive N.E., Suite 50
Tacoma, WA 98422
(206) 952-3285

69

Oakbridge University Press

Publishers of metaphysical books and materials.

The books that we publish reflect our desire to support and encourage the emerging consciousness of Light and Love, and to assist the awakening of all humanity to know the One Self that we truly are.

Jesus and Mastership
The Gospel According to Jesus of Nazareth
Channeled by James C. Morgan

The New Book of Revelation
From John the Disciple of Jesus the Christ
Channeled by James C. Morgan

Return Passage
A novel of reincarnation
By Michael Harvey

Wings To My Breath
Poetry of the Spirit's Quest
By Eva McGinnis

Remembrance
Healing Teachings and Stories
by Jeshua, David Hiller & Margaret Fuller Hiller

Shifting Into Miracle Thinking
David Hiller & Margaret Fuller Hiller

The Christmas Story: Remembrance
As told by Jeshua ben Joseph

Forthcoming:

The Personal Christ
Teachings of Jeshua ben Joseph
in expression with Judith Coates